The Apocalypse Came on a Friday

Haikus by Little John Nee

Published 2016 by Killaloonty Press

ISBN 978-0-9954853-0-3

Front Cover Photo: Paul McGuckin
Back Cover Photo: Laura Sheeran
Meadow illustration: Keeva Holland
Cover and Book Design: Paula Nolan
Printed by Browne Printers Ltd, Letterkenny, Co Donegal

While writing a play I
often use haiku to get to
the essence of a scene or
story, this becomes a daily
practice and over the years
I have accumulated a heap
of haiku.

I made a present to my
dear friend Keeva Holland,
a handwritten book of haiku
I thought she might like.
She suggested I publish
them. I suggested she
illustrate them. She had
just begun to do this when
she passed away. Her last
work was all about love. Her
compassion was one of the
most beautiful things
I have witnessed in my life.
I hope you can squeeze a bit
of goodness from this book. I
dedicate this book to her.

Day rich as butter
Heather beginning to bloom
Soft old punk writing

A beautiful sneeze
All over the computer
A sneezing haiku

Wee lamb exploring
Alone among the nettles
Never heard of mint sauce

The trees are like prints
On the cotton of white fog
On the hem of sky

Giddy as a pup
Snow and ice on the bog road
My heart full of song

I dance like a tramp
Shimmy, shuffle, soft shoe tap
In a big black coat

Pickled onion
Glasgow chip shop memory
Ah, the taste of words

Tea from India
Strong enough to trot a mouse
The way I like it

The tractor gearbox
    Disappearing under weeds
    Like a brooding hen

Old donkey jacket
Lost in the olive groves
The mountain is cold

Outside my wee house
White paint flakes in the sun
  Like cherry blossoms

  A shaft of sun
Thick with dancing dust
Like cattle swimming

The horseless meadow
   I discover my emptiness
     In this lush acre

This day like cold soup
   I would rather leave behind
   I put on my hat

Electricity
I light up like Jesus Christ
God's chosen juke box

Ah the bottle-bank
Sour smell of empty bottles
Narrative of glass

I see sheep grazing
And turn to write my haiku
Only one line left

Bright beautiful day
Vocabulary fails me
I can live with that

Crows walk through the snow
Approaching like commandos
Aware of danger

The apocalypse
Came on a Friday in March
It was not so bad

Brown speckled thrush
Hopping across the garden
Looking for breakfast

Loneliness and love
Little boy playing with string
A sunny garden

The uncertainty
The great cosmic mystery
A nice cup of tea

September Sunday
A visit to the graveyard
The appetite of clay

Giant dragonfly
Skims through the empty village
Hovering and gone

My ukulele
Handmade from mahogany
Sings like canaries

A happy biker
Gentle as an old lady
Rinsing a tea cup

A drunk man sleeping
Is woken by the bells
A lack of romance

Oily dungarees
He fumbles with the wheel nut
Sweet smelling old man

The tarmac melting
The sweet smell of diesel fumes
The sun shines on us

A noisy pigeon
  The cherry blossoms budding
  Season of growing

Rain drumming on tin
Galvanising my desire
I scribble a plan

Heavy summer rain
The school holidays begin
O the injustice

Independence Day
Americans celebrate
Their soldiers feel proud

I am very lost
I will sing a small song
And see what happens

Garden of roses
I play the ukulele
Watching ladybirds

Bathwater running
I live like an emperor
And still I want more

A wild wet morning
Imagination on fire
Cosy in my house

I would wish for love
    For that is the best of it
    As far as i see

The road to Galway
    And the Saturday market
    O happy routine

Savour the moment
Before I get out of bed
A small taste of bliss

Who am I today?
My jaw deep in shaving foam
Full of intention

Another wet day
But still it smells of summer
And that is enough

My car keys are lost
Where they are I do not know
Forever seeking

A slow moving cloud
Heading towards Roscommon
Across a blue sky

Lorry looks fucked
But with a bit of kindness
She might go again

Sore throat from singing
King of Donegal Voodoo
That's what they call me

He needs a new suit
Trawling the second hand shops
He might get lucky

O hurry hurry
No time to write a haiku
I have stuff to do

Disappearing men
The son hiding from the truth
The father dying

The dancing spanner
Hammer on the big oil drum
   Spring is in the barn

Well "hep" is the word
   The great timpani heartbeat
   Whole thing is swinging

Sometimes I do feel
Like a old dog on a rope
Not going nowhere

Light the pot belly
There is ice in the basin
As cold as your heart

Return to the pub
Perched precariously
On top of the hill

Black ice on the road
Nearly killed me before
I drive so so slow

This Hindu lady
In love with this Irishman
It beggars belief

In powder blue suit
A handsome ageing hepcat
From Caherlistrane

A dark moonless night
A big lorry spinning mud
Struggles up the hill

Wild wet bitter night
Driving up a muddy track
Shadow of a house

The house in darkness
So I grab an old blanket
And sleep in the truck

It was a hard day
But it is gone in the past
Where does it exist?

A rooster crowing
I climb out of my lorry
I go for a pee

Beyond the stone wall
Suspicious sheep stare at me
I am innocent

A distressed old pub
Sinking into the landscape
Half way up a hill

Men come here to die
Dead wasps on the window ledge
Thick dust on the glass

Unload the lorry
Sun drawing steam from the road
        Put up the marquee

        Dreams that perished
Their hungry ghosts come haunting
        And fill the wee pub

Let the good times roll
Let all the hurts be healed
Let you buy a drink

An old man running
Appears to be standing still
Drinking a whisky

I reverse the truck
I do not see the rooster
Till it is too late

The rooster is dead
I call to the caravan
We sit and drink tea

Hogs come up the hill
  Rumble like distant thunder
  Atmospheric change

Seven motorbikes
Seven motorbike riders
They met in rehab

Starlings on the wire
A man walks towards the pub
Dusk brings out the ghosts

Moonless summer night
There's a drunk in the farmyard
Looking for an axe

Sit down for a rest
At the side of the road
Listen to the birds

Sleep comes demanding
Dragging me down to dreamtown
To go carousing

Succulent meadows
Birds loud in every bush
Wild times in Leitrim

In an old tin shed
A young woman from Dublin
Finds a bicycle

Big black high nellie
Spinning wheels on rolling hills
Dazzled by hawthorn

Old bicycle shop
A hub of transportation
Where voyagers meet

Rescued from a skip
Dead flowers for a dead clown
Roses from Tralee

Filling water tanks
At a train stop in Pittsburgh
Looking at the moon

O my broken head
Sledge hammers on iron pegs
    Rise that tent gently

The devil with me
  Bad American whiskey
Rats and small monkeys

The smell of horses
The conversation of fools
And me sick from drink

Her two big eyeballs
The daughter of a horse thief
Annoying my head

Sick of the circus
    Sick of the circus people
    In need of a cure

Odd as a cowfish
But unremarkable here
    Where "in odd we trust"

Contrary as soap
In a bathtub of slapstick
A head full of fool

The tent is leaking
Rain dripping on the bandstand
The trombone gets wet

Promise of hard work
With small reward to follow
  Pulling on damp socks

Beat up and bruised
     He limps to the chuck wagon
     They can all see him

The band warming up
A trombone and a snare drum
Spreading the sawdust

A funny story
About two fools and a rat
Desperately sad

A woman passing
Another movie begins
In his busy mind

The quickening heart
The gravitational pull
The dance of nature

At my wooden desk
Face wet with salty tears
I mourn my mother

The wee broken song
They sing outside the café
Would lift a sore heart

Out for a small walk
        And perhaps to steal a tune
        From a singing bird

With my pork pie hat
        Leopard skin brothel creepers
        And Hawaii shirt

I lift up a stone
And then drop it on the road
Checking gravity

A story about
A man with a bag of queens
Driving to London

Below the primrose
In the poly-tunnel
    I find a fresh corpse

Butterfly resting
On a warm silver birch leaf
    No reason to fly

Grey as history
Wet as a brimming piss pot
The cold Bureaucrat

The blood on the floor
Is proving hard to remove
Better get carpet

Three people at work
A woman in dungarees
Tells it like it is

Hammering tent poles
Familiar rhythm ringing
Coffee on the boil

Here comes a hobo
With buckets of broken songs
Put on the kettle

Spanners and hammers
Wheels turning belts that turn wheels
Work that contraption

Administrator
  Frustrating my intention
    To be creative

The shame oh the shame
Find a rock to crawl under
  Isolate with pain

Walking in the rain
There is nothing else for it
  This is where I live

Down digging a hole
  In London in the winter
  I am not there now

I sing of gardens
Song of life loud in my heart
O happy swagger

The county chaos
You need your wits about you
To live in this place

Noisy bluebottle
Loudest thing in the whole world
Cannot ignore him

Banana sandwich
With highland heather honey
Toasted for breakfast

Today is Friday
February the thirteenth
But what does that mean?

The date and the day
Allegedly unlucky
Sad alligators

Doing tax returns
The Buddha of simple sums
Gently with a pen

Night time in Oldtown
Make haiku on a laptop
Letterkenny zen

Perrywinkle brain
Good words hide inside the shell
Haiku from a dream

Room full of dead flies
Bluebottles abandoned
Spider come tidy

Smell of engine oil
Ice on the puddles outside
Looking for jump leads

The new dynamo
On the old bicycle wheel
The bright beam of light

My father's last wish
    Is that the grass be cut
    So I cut the grass

We buried dad
    The day before yesterday
    We come and we go

The old parish hall
  Growing dark in the sunset
  With no electric

    Outside her wee house
  Feeding fish eyes to the hens
  Visions in her head

Back in the Oldtown
The house without my father
   The world so empty

Particles of dust
   Floating in infinity
     What has brought us here

Standing at the bar
His misery pronounced
Staring at the dog

If I had a horse
I'd jump on it and ride off
But I have no horse

O dear a dull day
        But not the end of the world
        Though it feels like it

A difficult day
My straitjacket is pinching
I sing a wee song

The mother of them
Beyond in Connemara
An ocean of love.

I open my mind
To the possibility
Of inspiration

Abundance of life
  Trees blossom and birds nest
  I am part of this

  As fresh as I was
Way back when I was so fresh
  I am fresher now

Laid on the sea shore
Blue as a Hindu goddess
On her seaweed bed

Patterns of dark thought
A ragged bunch of bandits
Pass through the village

No she is not dead
It has all been a mistake
She will be here soon

I hope for something
That will take away the pain
Of separation

Glasgow in springtime
Innocence and violence
Flirting in the street

Hunger of the soul
It may be I need breakfast
Very possibly

Holding the baby
Gliding around the kitchen
Dancing and singing

This is the parish
    Where the old man sat to rest
And never got up

I pack my suitcase
Shorts, socks, shirts and underwear
Everything I need

I spot a poster
The promoter bending the truth
Until it got broke

A herring bone suit
With creases like razorblades
Sharpest man in town

The field turns to mud
Rain rolling down the canvas
Bad day for a show

Working in the shed
An old man drops in for tea
A favour to ask

There are several ways
We can proceed with the job
Said the cat skinner

Nursing a sore head
Rain running down the tent flap
In need of fixing

Open the window
There are angels and old souls
Come to lend a hand

The pain of the shame
Of being broke and homeless
Make up excuses

The sabre rattle
Threatening blind violence
The drunken hussar

Empty in New York
With everything you want
    None of it enough

I got lost in town
    Too many pretty women
    I had to sit down

Desire drawing me
   Away from the wealth of now
   Promising much more

End of zero nine
Feel as dull as dishwater
   Roll on zero ten

Driving to Dublin
Through wind and rain and flooding
Why do I do this?

Emotional pain
Gutted by a rejection
Desire for revenge

Battle in my head
  Justifying the conflict
    Awake through the night

The smell of turf smoke
  An unexpected delight
  On a winter day

Back on the farm
 With a shovel in my hand
 Digging the summer

I walk down the lane
 Wondering at the conceit
 That took me away

Plumbing making noise
Writing in my fathers room
Face full of weeping

With songs and singing
The raw pain was chiseled
Sculpted to beauty

Fear on the tv
    Like sugar it gets me high
    And sticks to my teeth

I resolve today
    No crucifying myself
    Have a good Friday

Down at the roadside
Waiting for the wee red bus
Wet with spring showers

Do you remember
Postdramatic theatre?
Ah nostalgia

On St Patrick's Day
    Buddha statue in the rain
    Tolerant as stone

  If I were a crow
I would watch the man next door
  He has a shotgun

The stormy ocean
Of human experience
The calm of the soul

I seek innocence
Where it dwells inside of me
O simple science

O harmonium
Breathing like a drunk yogi
Some kind of special

These broken things
Scattered around the yard
Don't need mending

The dirt below me
    The gravity holding me
       From the dirt things grow

I am not feeling
  The bombs and unholy war
  I am not hungry